www.finishinglinepress.com

THE COLOR BETWEEN THE HOURS

poems by

Elizabeth Morse

Finishing Line Press
Georgetown, Kentucky

THE COLOR BETWEEN
THE HOURS

ACKNOWLEDGMENTS

Grateful thanks to the editors of the publications listed below:

"Psychic Hotline: Welfare to Work" originally appeared in *Lynx Eye.*
"Steep Weather" originally appeared in *Ship of Fools.*
"When It's Time to Retire, All Assets Will Be Toxic" appeared in slightly
different form in *Home Planet News.*
"The Nail Biting Cure" and "Nightshade" originally appeared in *Home Planet
News.*
"My Mother's Violin" appeared in slightly different form in *The Reading
Room.*
"The Man I Knew Too Well" originally appeared in *Downtown Poets
Anthology.*
"When You Left" originally appeared in *Wavelength.*
"Expressway" originally appeared in *Hazmat Review.*
"Injuries of Heaven," "Microwave Horoscope and Palm Reading," "True
Crime" and "Unreasonable Weather" originally appeared in *Ginosko*
"On the Outskirts" originally appeared in *Survision.*
"Oracle of Lost Cats" originally appeared in *The Headlight Review* and *The
2022 Brownstone Poets Anthology.*

Publisher: Leah Huete de Maines
Editor: Christen Kincaid
Cover Art: Kathleen McArdle
Author Photo: Linda Kleinbub
Cover Design: Elizabeth Maines McCleavy

Order online: www.finishinglinepress.com
also available on amazon.com

Author inquiries and mail orders:
Finishing Line Press
PO Box 1626
Georgetown, Kentucky 40324
USA

Table of Contents

In loving memory of Travis Alexander Freeman

THE NAIL-BITING CURE

My arms are stumps because I bite my nails.
I look great, like Venus de Milo.
My father warned me about this and
I refused to believe him.

Sleep comes haltingly, gasping for breath in
the apnea of surprise, the heat of supercharged
lightning. I strike out laughing, barely conscious,
with sticks and can-openers.
I have no need, I say. I can keep going
all night, thoughts buzzing into mirages.
The moon eggs me on.
That is just your trouble, the doctors say.

Fear is not the chopper with the searchlight.
It is accusing voices on the phone hissing and
ranting. You deserve this, they say.
With absolute power, fear shouts from billboards,
detonates movie-like explosions in yellow
and orange. Fear hides in white sound.
Drops of blood spoil the white carpet.
How dare you!

You ask if I have any faults.
So many blips I can't talk about:
speedy words, endless night without stars,
unmovable clutter of books and papers,
quenchless thirst unmoved by Gatorade,
bugs in the brain, perfumes from long ago.
But it's time to answer, and I do.

MICROWAVE HOROSCOPE AND PALM READING

Avoid the path of romance, of shooting stars
so that you wind up alone at home, touching the numbers
to make hot lunch in April, chicken soup with rice.
The currency of fate must not be spent on carnivals,
or fried chicken with coleslaw in a silver-lined bag.

Tonight's dinner must be irradiated.
Your palm lines show an acute sense of smell and taste.
No COVID here. Tea leaves dance in a glass.
You miss the silver-lined bag you used to bring home.
It's supermarket delivery now, groceries left at the door.
Dump out green beans from plastic.
Add sage to pasta in a blue china plate that will turn
in light. Tiny portions bode well for long life.

Your horoscope slings the weight of the past directly
into a future of sundial cooking instructions.
You'll be solitary forever in a plague-ridden world.
Thawed chocolate mousse will be eaten by candlelight
with a dainty spoon, one damask cloth napkin.
Rune stones turn up blank as you finger them,
portending not death for you but total change.
Radiant tarot cards tell the same.
Your mother's hand showed a short life and hospital stay.
Did the zodiac design doom on the ones who were gasping?
Did some vindictive psychic know and not tell all?
Was it all configured beforehand in the astral world?
Fate means cooking alone with the hum of the box,
means never hefting casseroles for visits home.
Patterns of love are voided by cruelty of inescapable stars.
An egg blows up, leaving streaks on the microwave window.

PSYCHIC HOTLINE: WELFARE TO WORK

As of January 26, 2000, the NYC Welfare Department was providing training for welfare recipients to work as telephone psychics.

The future is green.
Thick lawns and emeralds pave the way.
Getting off Welfare, you can use your dreams
to ignite the dreams of others, fan the flames
burning past brick walls and fences.
Best job you ever had.
All you have to do is talk on the phone.
Massive highways, trips around the world:
you will meet someone shortly.
Behind the lamppost in the middle of the street
a short-stemmed beauty, overflowing
bleached white hair and pow pink lipstick.
Garbage cans overflow with Styrofoam.
The future is white and soiled. Littered with
the beer cans of your old neighborhood.
Never again. The future is what counts,
counts toward gray-green paper with
pictures of pyramids and long-gone presidents.
Who knows what liberties they took?
The future is red, dotted with rubies, lit with lasers.
beautiful blood in vials, dark wine in smoky bottles
Tomato stew is in the pot, enough to feed all five children.
Tell them anything. Tell them what they want to hear.
But don't tell them off.

STEEP WEATHER

The darkened windows of your house flirt with light.
Your cell phone hollows words,
guts the richness of your voice,
your accent, slashes whole phrases.

I dream of maps to find you with,
blue highways for the car
I don't yet know how to drive.

You drove past vanishing, over bridges,
into tunnels that day, not knowing
you would disappear.
If you'd reached your destination: the towers,
leaking smoke, furniture and people
who got to work on time. Fate, you tell me.

Neither of us wanted to be alone in the wounded city.
Our words flew from torn circles and twisted steel.
Filling in darkened windows, I reach for chunks of light.
It's late, you say. I think of maps and shifting sunsets.
You were born in Ankara.
I don't even know your first language.

Under lofty ceilings, I think of your fierce brown eyes.
Together, we watch the thunder, our words gliding,
found, if just for an instant. I do not want to be
pried from your hands.

The candle smokes, tilting precariously.
Lightning takes the sky.
I pray for an easy rain.

INJURIES OF HEAVEN

In my dream, you were waiting for me in a booth.
Crinkly paper placemats, the old-style ones,
put me in mind of road trips with my parents,
though we were in Manhattan near West Fourth.
You told me how she didn't drink like I did,
so you left, drunk yourself, your plaid shirt stained,
saying you were going out for cigarettes.
You drifted across prairies in a Plymouth Duster,
matches used up, pack long empty.
You were always going to leave New York,
that arcane land of vertical spaces.
I think of her long hair in the photo I found,
a thick blonde curtain, light eyes, skin translucent paper.
My vagrant love, did you still want to talk to me?
The delicates of long ago have shredded with age.

Your kinetic eyes gleam at four in the morning.
I put on sweats to make you red cabbage
to go with dirty beer. I'd hardly make it to work.
But there we'd sit, curled on the sofa, laughing,
listening to Peter Gabriel, neighbors knocking
as you traced desire around my hips,
We prayed for steady weather.

We ate sandwiches at the diner, the kind on wispy toast,
resurrected from fried chicken, ketchup, and chopped beef.
You got one of those foreign beers you never liked.
I ordered the coffee I had to.
You set down your feet in gray boots,
cowboy patterns carved into the sides.
The veil is thin now, before passing into November.
Didn't know how many conscious days I had left, you say,
putting your hand over mine.
You knew there'd never be a miracle.

TRUE CRIME

What you said at 4 AM
A cone of light on the sheets
Stacks of unopened envelopes
You say a probation officer
That's what you've got
Black hair curls over your ears
In past lives, we married others
Dreams blow through windows
That's why you left Houston
A thump on the door
A naked startle
Glasses half full of whiskey
It's nothing, you say
It's everything, I tell you
A rent check forged
A solid Brooklyn day is coming
You will or won't go back
I will twist the lock
Until it explodes
I cut out the light
Until I can't

PAYING ATTENTION

I painted my walls white
so I can really listen
to the clocktick workings,
cars gliding on patent leather streets.
Black and white tiles
in the kitchen of childhood.
I think back to chandeliers and foxfur,
holding out my hands for carved faces
over tenement doorways.
I never left my old neighborhood
though I sit at a desk miles south
shielded from rain like bits of glass.

NIGHTSHADE

Tomatoes are nightshade.
Toxins have been lurking in our salad.
My friend pointed out dark berries.
Deadly Nightshade, she said,
the fruit of malicious desserts,
the tomatoes of pupil dilation.
Each restaurant serves red half-moons
that taste like gravelly ice.

Nightshade berries taste like love, my friend said.
Someone tired of a spouse could make
a fabulous dinner, luring their former beloved
into another kind of bed.

For seven-year-olds who want to make poison
there are antidotes on kitchen shelves.
The children eat tomatoes for lunch at school
though no one goes home sick.

Everyone has wanted to poison someone sometime.

MY MOTHER'S VIOLIN

I see you as a child, hands in pockets,
standing in front of a house on an impossible hill,
round face framed by harsh straight hair.
Did you imagine me then, did you know
you would pull me out of your pocket
in just over twenty years?

I am thinking of violin melodies,
the half-size instrument you played
with plump fingers too young to hold a pen.
The space between the notes is too great,
allowing grief to seep through stone.
This is what you don't believe in,
preferring the gray only you and
my father ever knew. It's low-cost
color chosen by proud socialists
who moved to a high-rise
on the edge of Harlem in 1959.

Your hands were always soft.
Your shame, perhaps, not to be leathery enough
by the taut bow, the catgut strings.
Your darling's curved wood body fills
the lacks in your blue desire.
You were my first love;
I could not endure.

My grandmother's pearl handled revolver
shooed you out, took you to New York
for graduate school. The closest to divorce
was her locked room, the gun in her drawer.
My grandfather lurked when he got back from jail.
The violin's curvy body melted
in your embrace, long after your parents
had vanished behind the windows of Greyhound.
Your loneliness, carried forward, astounds me.

BLUE ROADS

Neon signs explode the night
with come-ons pointing to needs
I don't want to have.
I dream of highways to reach you,
maps of interweaving lines
leading to a paradise of gingerbread houses
that never belonged anywhere near here.

I will never go back
along the old routes, past bare trees
auto boneyards, trailer parks.
My great grandfather is buried in
the side of a mountain with only
a rutted path to get there.

I am lost on the interstate afraid
of not finding the right exit
leading to your house, my distant love.
Your face comes to me when I least expect.
When I am in the mountains
hundreds of miles away,
close to dense trees and twisty roads.

I see stars in a quiet, wooded world, hoping
I'd see you on the porch of a house
you've never been to, hoping you'll be there
right after dawn,
saying you drove all night to reach me.

EXPRESSWAY

He pulls up in an SUV, pushing open the door.
"Get in," he says, and you do, fearing
a wavery life you can't depend on.
Sky and highway liquefy,
rolling off the printed page.

The city doesn't treat you well anymore.
Infidelities blink from every streetcorner.
It's time to learn to drive, even at fifty,
venturing out on the expressway,
away from oppressive rooms.

Outsized green road signs tell you you're lost.
Wobbly-fat, you squeeze behind the wheel.
He's in the back seat now. No pastures are left,
only strip-malls and billboards.
All you can do is keep going,
past swamps, water-towers,
and for the first time ever, free.

THE MAN I KNEW TOO WELL

Shadows on your face
tell me you have other lives,
lottery tickets bought in haste,
hidden in drawers, never checked.
Do you want to be twenty again,
head covered in coarse dark hair
like a werewolf's? You were fiercer
and proud of it.
I really was dangerous, you say,
and smile. The intervening years,
complete with plumbers and psychiatrists,
have smoothed you, worn you down
into someone else. When I say
you are rich, you shake your head,
not wanting to translate
the coarseness of your insides
into ornate tin ceilings and draperies.
The wood paneling is more genteel
than you'd like.
It's disinformation, you say,
shaking your head vigorously,
though it's Anglo-Saxon words
you're looking for,
the ones you can't make
yourself pronounce.
You pour a drink, a single-malt scotch,
and dream of incinerating all your books,
marble sculptures, your late-in-life treasures.

HAUNTED

This is your house:
your mother's things from another time,
shoe boxes, round tortoiseshell glasses,
belt with flower buckle,
artifacts to weigh us down,
circular fluorescent light over the table,
cracking paint, the climb to the attic.
Nightly, I see myself there.

From the house I hear a distant train.
I am leaving the upstairs bedroom,
the blue lounge chair,
creaky cellar stairs,
tiffany lampshade,
the orange cat
meowing in the kitchen.

In thunder we go to your car.
Shadow station looms ahead.
You buy my ticket,
handing it off at the last moment.
I am alone in my seat, pulling away.
The train passes a bridge dotted with light.
A woman looks at her phone and laughs.
Outside the window, the river glitters.

I am leaving the linoleum covered stairs,
the blue lounge chair,
circular fluorescent light over the table.
We say each other's names,
watch flickering images of CNN.
It is our house together, but not.

WHEN YOU LEFT

the streets were flooded.
Someone paddled a canoe down Wall Street.
Dead newspaper flew against windows.
Beggars collected piles of cans and shook
them while sitting in life preservers.
Was anything worth saving?

When you left, I went back to the old house,
the inescapable rooms with ceaseless melodies
woven by piano and clarinet.
Haunted houses never leave me, especially at night.
The walls leak ancient
fluids, dripping into cisterns of the too-early morning.

When you left, I read stories of cannibals.
Who would have thought the peaceful Anasazi
would resort to eating flesh?
After that, I stopped remembering what it felt like.
It's just that what we don't want to know
seeps into our fingers, tears our skin at night.

THE SNOW QUEEN

Silver bells float from the ceiling.
The gap between trees doesn't close.
Wind blows through your ribcage
as her perfect fingers grip your wrist,
peeling off silver beads and gloves.

She holds your hand in frigid water, saying,
this is how we wash our clothes.
The promise of a snowbound world
yawns directly in front of you.
Tiny, sleepy windows snap shut.

Her assistant strokes the harp after midnight,
enchanted icicles tinkle faintly.
She kisses your forehead, so you won't know
how thick the ice is around you.
Will everything end like this?

HALF-LIFE

Swallowing shadows nightly at five o'clock,
I am surrounded by swirling dust,
lives flattened like printed cardboard,
stale as ashtrays.
It's the smoky taste that counts.
The rest is too hard to knock against.

Weightiness frightens, presses me into daylight.
The light is too white to breathe.
Better go indoors, finding whiskey,
expanding artificial light,
gold-embossed leather books,
convincing us of manufactured holiness.

When you look into my face,
I know I am not the one. If I were,
I'd lose seclusion in rooms that never open.
I'm glad no one sees too clearly.
So, I can be who I want.
It doesn't matter that lilies wilt in my home.

Every sound cuts flesh, dislodges brick.
Two people to put you here, and one to leave.
The young girl's journey is over.
It's time to sit back and drink.
Only brocades are beautiful now.
Still, they vanish way too soon.

FOR YOUR OWN SAFETY

Suddenly, the robbery begins,
the thieves with cut-out red socks over their faces.
All they need is a crowbar for the front door.
Our neighbor goes on practicing the trumpet.
The alarm clicks not once but twice to turn off.
The safe code is obvious:
the letters are painted on the front door.
You never know about these attacks.
When they happen, they happen.

The past is another land with a low crime rate.
People use a different alphabet,
painting carefully with brushes and feather-pens.
Takes time to learn.
By the time you're done, the present sneaks in.
My toddler son stands on the steps, smiling.
This photo has crisp edges that shred with
unreasonable weather.
I cannot understand the shapes,
though they once surrounded me.
Heavy glass doors won't let me back in.

My home's unsafe even though I paid
half my salary for an alarm.
The stove spurts flame but does not deter burglars.
I am tired of being invaded, tired of broken bricks.
It's a good day when the sky doesn't rain ashes.

ORACLE OF LOST CATS

They talk to me, tell me of their loves.
It isn't what they say, it's how they chase us.
I see the ones no one else does,
tabbies, tiny panthers, Bengals that look like leopards,
the white ones with one blue and one golden eye.
They vanish in the stumbling city. Cars honk.
The motors are warm but treacherous hiding places.
The cats dream of sky and birds, what all of us want:
imagine moving upwards in those intricate branches.
climbing down isn't the same as climbing up.

Signs go up in the neighborhood,
tales of silly names, rough attachment.
They get spooked, impressed by wild sounds.
I know where your cat is.
She does not understand how she is driven
by past scents, perfume of meat.
Long ago is a sidewalk not taken now.
There is only the way back.
Open a can.

UPTOWN, NEAR THE RIVER

Gravy in potatoes under a ceiling of chalky paint,
lighted dimly by sconces with frozen candle bulbs.
Aunts and uncles bicker in the next room.
Tomorrow, the girl will be home again
with blocky parents in drafty blue-gray rooms.
Her aunt who lives here will perish in a cloud
of radiator steam, stabbed by a short-term boyfriend
using a steak knife from an unstuck drawer.
None of the relatives will see the blood or grainy photos.
She was too trusting, they'll say.
The heat in the apartment softened her like gelatin.
The girl, slightly older, will marvel at how her aunt
lived to stir lumps out of coffee-colored gravy.

UNREASONABLE WEATHER

Rain pounds the windows.
It is not enough that rent is due,
that people take off during the night
driving through mud to soup kitchens.
No work in months.
Wind tears chunks from hillsides.
The yard is flooded, littered with toys.
You are ill, a mother says,
adjusting her mask
and her child's.
Can you walk to the door?
We have to leave.
A determined cat swims downriver,
past steep waterfalls thick with sound.
A dog cries in the back of an SUV.
Ambulances swoosh through puddles,
sirens on. Inside, breath is stilted.
The hospitals are full.
Some house doors are left open,
others nailed shut.
Trees split and fall.
Love and loss are tidal,
basic as the rocks.

WHEN IT'S TIME TO RETIRE, ALL ASSETS WILL BE TOXIC
A Tritina in memory of Stephen Mohr, a friend and coworker

Retirement is obsolete, you told me, bankruptcy's the work of the future.
Surrounded by empty seats, we lounged in swivel chairs, each in a cubicle,
testing funds transfer systems, fluorescent light haunting the ceiling and walls.

We fall down tired as we age, defeating old angers, ruining the safety of walls.
You hadn't worked in over a year. Robber barons took all, aiming for the future.
I got the message about your memorial service while lingering late in my cubicle.

You were looking for clues, rooting around the desk drawers in your cubicle,
empty store windows, the Federal Reserve castles, picketing of Wall Street's walls,
announcing the world's end, crowds out of work, pushing against the future.

Released, you drift through walls, above the bankrupt cubicle that cannot be your future now.

ON THE OUTSKIRTS

Walking past stone pillars,
you touch your forehead to water.
The coolness of staying in one place
takes the wonder of everything away.
You get used to it in small towns.
People forget what they did years ago,
pulling the hands off clocks,
the glass out of windows.
No forgiveness is good enough.
People you know don't really believe, anyway.
In the yard, a swimming pool inflates.
The dusty sleep of people living in the house
is what you inhale at night.
Leaving here is what terrifies you.

Elizabeth Morse is a poet who lives in New York's East Village. Her work has been published in literary magazines such as *Blue Mesa Review, Hazmat Review, Lynx Eye,* and *Freezer Burn,* and anthologies such as *Crimes of the Beats* and *The Unbearables Big Book of Sex.* Her poetry chapbook, *The Future Is Now,* was published by Linear Arts Press. She was a finalist in the Blue Light Press full-length poetry collection contest and has her MFA from Brooklyn College. A job in information technology supports her writing.

www.ingramcontent.com/pod-product-compliance
Lightning Source LLC
Chambersburg PA
CBHW022107080426
42734CB00009B/1509

*9 7 9 8 8 8 8 3 8 4 1 9 0 *